I See a Tiger

Written by Marie Gabriel

Illustrated by Gustavo Mazali

Teacher's Edition written by Kay Kovalevs

Say

'Let's read page 2 together. Then look at the illustration.'

Read

Read page 2 together with the students, and ask them to look at the illustration.

Check Understanding

- Where is the girl?
- What is the girl doing?
- What word is the opposite of the word 'asleep'?

Talk

How do you think the character felt on this page?

I **think** the **character** felt _____.

Why do you think this?

I **think** this because the text told me _____ and the **illustration** told me _____.

Say

'Read page 4 to your partner. Then ask your partner to read page 4 to you.'

Read

Ask pairs of students to take it in turns to read page 4 to each other.

Check Understanding

- What does the girl see?
- In the illustration, what does the shadow on the wall look like?

Talk

Do you think that there really is a tiger in the house?

I **think** that _____.

Why do you think this?

I **think** this because _____.

How do you think the girl felt at this moment in the story?

I **think** the girl **felt** _____ at this moment in the **story**.

Say

'Read page 6 by yourself and look at the illustration. What does it tell you?'

Read

Ask the students to read page 6 silently to themselves, and to think about what the illustration tells them.

Check Understanding

- Was the shadow a tiger?
- What caused the shadow?
- In the illustration, what is the girl doing?

Talk

How do you think the girl is feeling now?

I **think** that the girl is feeling _____.

How do you know this?

I know this because _____.

What do you think the author wants us to know about the character of the girl in the story?

I **think** the author wants us to know that the **character** in the **story** _____.

Say

'Read page 8 silently to yourself. Then read it aloud. What is in the illustration?'

Read

Ask the students to read page 8 silently, then aloud. Encourage them to think about what the illustration shows.

Check Understanding

- What does the girl see?
- Where is the kitten hiding?

Talk

What clues on this page tell you how the character is feeling?

The **character** is feeling _____.
The clues in the **illustration** are _____.

Do you think that there is really a dinosaur in the story?

I **think** _____ in the **story**.

How do you know?

I know this because _____.

Say

'Take turns to read page 10 to your partner. What characters are on page 11?'

Read

Ask pairs of students to take it in turns to read page 10 to each other. They should talk to each other about which characters are on page 11.

Check Understanding

- Was it a dinosaur?
- What was the shadow?

Talk

How do you think the character felt when she realised the shadow was a hat? Why?

I **think** the **character felt** _____.
I know this because the **illustration** shows _____.

What do you think the cat is thinking?

I **think** that the cat _____.

Why do you think this?

I **think** this because _____.

Say

'Let's read page 12 together.'

Read

Read page 12 together with the students.

Check Understanding

- What does the girl see?
- In the illustration, how many fingers has the monster got?

Talk

What do you think is making the shadow on the wall?

I **think** that _____.

What do you think this story is about?

I **think** this **story** is **about** _____.

Why do you think this?

I **think** this because the text and illustrations tell me _____.

Say

'Read this page together with a partner. What is the illustration telling you?'

Read

Ask the students to read page 14 together with their partner. They should talk about what the illustration tells them.

Check Understanding

- It's not a monster. Who is it?
- In the illustration, where is the girl?

Talk

What was the funniest part of this story?

The funniest part of this **story** was _____.

What do you think the author wants us to think about?

I **think** the author wants us to **think about** _____.

After Reading

Let's Think About It

- Have you ever been scared of a shadow at night?
- Imagine that you did see a shadow. What would it look like? How would you feel?
- What did you learn from reading this book?

Let's Talk About It

Turn to your partner and discuss your answers.

- At night, I …
- If I saw a shadow, I think it would look like … I think I would feel …
- I learned …

How are your answers the same or different?